The Layman's Bible Study
Series

Understanding John 3:16 & John 14:6

By Jim Melanson

Understanding John 3:16 & John 14:6

The Layman's Bible Study Series, Book 2

© 2017 by James Melanson

Distributed by CreateSpace.Com and Amazon.Com

ISBN: 978-0-9949203-6-2

More titles available at:
www.jimmelanson.ca

Editorial service provided by Dorathy Gass
www.metwritingservices.com

Cover graphic licensed from iStockPhoto.Com.

Scripture is taken from THE HOLY BIBLE, NEW INTERNATIONAL VERSION®, NIV® Copyright

APA Style Citation:

Melanson, J. (May 09, 2017). *The Layman's Bible Study Series: Understanding John 3:16 & John 14:6*. [eBook] Cobourg, ON

Dedication

This book is dedicated to my mother and father, Jackie Ryder and Edward "Eddie" Melanson. They set many examples for me and formed much of who I am. My mother's demonstration of faith in God which persisted through a difficult life was an inspiration. Very late in her life I realised that it was her faith in God that kept her going; that kept her smiling; that simply kept her.

When I was thirteen, I was baptised. At that time my father, a Catholic, converted to the Christian faith so that he and I could be baptised on the same day. This was an expression not only of his love for God, but his love for me as well. I still remember sitting in the pre-baptismal Bible study with several teens, and my father. He looked awkward and out of place, but he put himself there. I've always been impressed with how eloquently that simple, hardworking man answered the minister's questions.

Mom and Dad, this one is for you.

Your example was not lost on me.

Introduction

As a Christian, my life has been changed because of God's love, Jesus' sacrifice, and the presence of the Holy Spirit. My life has become one of peace, reassurance, and calmness over the life that I used to lead B.G. (Before God). I will witness to anyone that wants to hear, and sometimes to those who don't. When I do, I speak of the peace and love that God has filled my life with. I tell people how he didn't remove all the challenges, but he made those I still experience to be eminently more bearable by walking with Him.

Being filled with hatred, recrimination, and distrust is tiring — *it wears on you*. It makes everything less enjoyable. Entropy may be the natural state of our physical bodies, but not for our soul. When you truly give your life to God, put your life in his hands, develop a relationship with Him, and honestly allow yourself to love Him — the transformation you will experience inside is incredible. It is something that you can only truly understand when you experience it.

It doesn't mean that I don't still have challenges. It doesn't mean that I don't still have to work to overcome sin. It doesn't mean that everything is coming up roses. What it means is that I know I can face all of these things with a quiet assurance that on the far side, I will come out exactly where He wants me to be. It means that as I walk through those minefields of life, I do so with the confidence and calmness of the Holy Spirit moving within me, and God moving beside me. Regardless of all the challenges I have had to deal with, with Him by my side I have *always* come out in a better place or circumstance.

So, I have to ask myself, "Why do so many professed Christians get God's love wrong?"

I know that I am going to upset a lot of people with this book, and I'm okay with that. You can't please everyone. For far too long, some Christians have followed the loudest as though they were right. Unfortunately, louder isn't always right. That same thought goes for the atheists and agnostics: *louder isn't always right.*

I know that I'm one small voice speaking out for God alongside the dogma, doctrine, and misunderstanding of many others. Yet, I still hope that it will encourage a change for the betterment of the world. I'm comforted by the words of Elie Wiesel, a Nobel-Prize-winning writer, teacher, activist, and Holocaust survivor:

"We must always take sides. Neutrality helps the oppressor, never the victim.

Silence encourages the tormentor, never the tormented."

I have to speak out; I can't be silent anymore — and my views may never be fully accepted, but I hope they will make people think more critically and with more emotional intelligence about their faith, about salvation, and about what God wants from us *and* for us. That is what I want from this book, to make people think for themselves. I can no longer conscience the hatred, vitriol, and egoism derived from self-serving interpretations of the gospels.

I watch the news and see the hatred of Westboro Baptist Church (WBC), and it makes me want to cry. This group rejoices and celebrates when soldiers are killed doing their job, and when police officers die in the line of duty[1]. They express thankfulness for 9/11[2]. They have even threatened to protest the funeral of children killed at Sandy Hook Elementary School (2012), but thankfully they failed to show[3]. That doesn't change the angst they caused by their threats. In 2013, this organisation planned to protest at the funeral of 9-

year-old Scott McCabe of Owasso, Oklahoma, who was killed during a tornado[4].

Writing specifically about Westboro Baptist Church, American First Amendment scholar David Hudson Jr. writes[5]:

"The church's more recent protests unleashed a torrent of legislative activity rarely rivaled in the annals of First Amendment history. More than 40 states and the U.S. Congress have passed laws limiting funeral protests — largely as a direct result of the Westboro Baptist Church. Many municipalities have also passed funeral-protest ordinances at the local level."

WBC isn't the only group out there preaching hatred, contrary to God's message of love. Abiding Truth Ministries' service called DefendTheFamily.com is an anti-gay organisation that is openly hateful. The American Family Association conducts public protests against transgender people[6].

Kingdom Identity Ministries preaches a message of white supremacy[7]: *Kingdom Identity Ministries is a Politically Incorrect Christian Identity outreach ministry to God's chosen race (true Israel, the White, European peoples).*

The organization America's Promise Ministries also preaches a racially-biased message[8]: *Follow the studies, sermons and various books and pamphlets contained herein that prove that the Anglo-Saxon, Germanic, Scandinavian People are the descendants of Abraham, Isaac, and Jacob and that they are God's instruments to bring forth the True Gospel to all the earth.*

I can assure you, there is nothing "Godly" or "Christian" about the actions of these groups or any other group that uses God as justification for their hatred. Any alleged Christian group that publicly condemns a group of people for being different have it wrong. The reasons their actions are wrong are clearly laid out in The Bible.

Proverbs 6:16-19 - "There are six things the Lord hates, seven that are detestable to him: haughty eyes, a lying tongue, hands that shed innocent blood, a heart that devises wicked schemes, feet that are quick to rush into evil, a false witness who pours out lies and a person who stirs up conflict in the community." (NIV)

Matthew 6:14-15 - "For if you forgive other people when they sin against you, your heavenly Father will also forgive you. But if you do not forgive others their sins, your Father will not forgive your sins." (NIV)

John 8:7 - "And as they continued to ask him, he stood up and said to them, "Let him who is without sin among you be the first to throw a stone at her." (NIV)

Romans 12:19 - "Do not take revenge, my dear friends, but leave room for God's wrath, for it is written: "It is mine to avenge; I will repay," says the Lord." (NIV)

Too much suffering, too much strife, and too much pain has been brought into this world "… in Jesus' name" or "… in the name of God." As a somewhat intelligent and reasonable person, I know that this is not what He intended. What God wants from us is for us to love one another (e.g.: 1 John 4:7-8; John 13:34-35).

To put a point on this, there are two passages in the Bible that are misunderstood because people aren't paying attention to what they are reading. These two passages are:

John 3:16 - For God so loved the world that he gave his only Son, that whoever believes in him shall not perish but have eternal life. (NIV)

John 14:6 - Jesus answered, "I am the way and the truth and the life. No one comes to the Father except through me." (NIV)

With this book, I plan to challenge what some people understand about these two passages, and show why properly understanding them would have prevented much of the aforementioned "bad news". It is my desire and hope that after reading these pages, you will hold on to the "good news" of the Gospel of John that these two passages bring, not just to Christians, but to everyone in the world.

Are these the only misunderstood passages? Heck no! But these two passages are the focus of this book. Perhaps, if people come to truly understand the intention of these passages, not just their isolated literal interpretation, then that critical thinking and emotional intelligence will bleed over to how a person reads and understands the Bible to begin with.

For now, though, I ask just that you keep an open mind until you get to the end of the book. Then you need to take a close look at your own beliefs and feelings on the topics presented. The purpose of the book is not to tell you what to think; the purpose of this book is to give you a way to understand based on the words before you, rather than blindly following pulpit dogma.

What is my authority?

I don't have any college or university degrees in biblical studies, though I am studying biblical topics with an online Christian university.

I've been with a large metropolitan police service for close to thirty years. I hold a position that manages a large group of people in an operational setting, though I am not a police officer. My job is to listen, to watch, to evaluate, and to often make snap decisions that affect the welfare and safety of people. I have training in critical thinking, conflict resolution, and leadership.

For several years, I had my own business writing software. While I'm no longer formally involved in that pursuit, I do still use that technical expertise of problem-solving and logical analysis.

For over twenty years of my adult life, I walked in the darkness without God's light. This was not because God took the light away, it was because I turned my back on God. In my 20's I made the decision to reject God, Jesus, Christianity, the Bible, and the Holy Spirit. The 'why' is unimportant, the fact that I found my way back *is* important. During this dark period of my life, I was involved in the occult, paganism, witchcraft; beliefs and practices that would shock you. In 2011, with my life yet again on the brink of destruction, a friend said to me, "Perhaps it's time to let go, and let God."

That day I apologised to God and confessed my sins to Him. I opened my heart and my life to Him, inviting God to come back in. Since then, my life has improved dramatically, and it has been filled with daily blessings. Since that day, I've walked with God at my side and never had any doubt about His reality, or that He exists, because of the powerful effects His presence has had on me. I've developed and continue to develop that relationship with Him through reading the Bible, prayer, and loving my fellow man. There are many times since those dark days that God has carried me through troubling times. In learning how that felt, I realised that during the twenty-plus years that I had turned my back on God, He never turned His back on me. As I looked back over that period of darkness, I could see His hand at work, saving me and guiding me, though I refused to acknowledge his presence.

So, to answer the question, "What is my authority?" I would have to say that I have no authority, I simply have my love for God; I simply have a desire to both understand his word and share that understanding with others, and I have the ability to apply criticality and emotional intelligence to my understanding of scripture.

Chapter 1

Why do we believe the Gospel of John?

Before we delve into the subject matter of this book, it's important that we understand where these passages are coming from, and what the authority is that we give these passages in the Gospel of Salvation, the New Testament Gospel of John.

The four Canonical Gospels of the Bible's New Testament are written after the death of Jesus. The first three Gospels (Matthew, Mark, and Luke) are called the *Synoptic Gospels*, as they are very similar in content, structure, and voice. The term *synoptic* means 'with the same eye' or 'seeing together.' These three Gospels convey the story of Jesus' life. Are these three Gospels exhaustive? No, absolutely not. They relate the events that the authors felt inspired to convey.

As with almost every item of religious or biblical interest, there is controversy over whether or not the fourth gospel, the Gospel of John, was written by John bar-Zebedee (brother of James), an apostle of Christ. An exploration of this controversy can be found in an article by Mark P. Shea, a popular Catholic writer and speaker, in the Catholic.com online magazine. His conclusion is that the Apostle John published this Gospel at Ephesus in the second half of the first century[9]. However, that is only one opinion. The growing attitude I have found in my research seems to be that the Gospel of John, in addition to the Synoptic Gospels, are considered to be anonymous.

I know that quoting Bart Ehrman will be contentious for some readers, but this is a contentious book to begin with. I do have a reason for doing so.

Bart Ehrman, Professor in the Department of Religious Studies at the University of North Carolina explains the problems relating to the identification of the authorship regarding the four gospels[10]:

"The four Gospels... are all anonymous, written in the third person about Jesus and his companions. None of them contains a first-person narrative ("One day, when Jesus and I went into Capernaum..."), or claims to be written by an eyewitness or companion of an eyewitness. Why then do we call them Matthew, Mark, Luke and John? Because sometime in the second century, when proto-orthodox Christians recognized the need for apostolic authorities, they attributed these books to apostles (Matthew and John) and close companions of apostles (Mark, the secretary of Peter; and Luke, the travelling companion of Paul). Most scholars today have abandoned these identifications, and recognize that the books were written by otherwise unknown but relatively well-educated Greek-speaking (and writing) Christians during the second half of the first century."

In Ehrman's book *Forged*, he states[11]:

"Justin Martyr, writing around 150-60 CE, quotes verses from the Gospels, but does not indicate what the Gospels were named. For Justin, these books are simply known, collectively, as the 'Memoires of the Apostles.' It was about a century after the Gospels had been originally put in circulation that they were definitively named Matthew, Mark, Luke, and John. This comes, for the first time, in the writings of the church father and heresiologist Irenaeus, around 180-85 CE."

We can see from these two different sources that authorship of the gospels is a question that is not settled, and probably never will be. However, lack of concrete identification of the gospels' authorship does not affect their reliability.

William Lane Craig, Research Professor of Philosophy at Talbot School of Theology, and Professor of Philosophy at Houston Baptist

University has several arguments as to why the gospels remain reliable, as opposed to focusing on their authorship. Ultimately, Professor Craig says[12]:

Finally, when you think about it, the names of the Gospels' authors are quite immaterial. At most what matters is that the author, whether named Luke or Joshua or Herkimer or what have you, was in a position to deliver historically reliable information about the historical Jesus …

… having some knowledge of the Gospels' authors can, indeed, be helpful. But the point remains: it's not crucial.

Another reason for us to accept the reliability of the four Canonical Gospels is the sheer amount of writings that are not part of the New Testament. Groups of writings known as the infancy gospels, Jewish-Christian gospels, sayings gospels, Gnostic texts, Leucian Acts, non-canonical epistles, the apocalypses, etc. were all rejected from canonization of the New Testament because their contents could either not be verified, or were not trusted.

Without delving into the extensive topic of textual criticism, I will put forward that there is abundant evidence and reason to believe in the authenticity and reliability of the four Canonical Gospels of the

New Testament. If you would like to learn more about the evidentiary process of accepting these works, I would recommend you start with *A Student's Guide to Textual Criticism of the Bible: Its History, Methods & Results* by Paul D. Wegner (2006), Intervarsity Press, ISBN: 0830827315.

How the Gospel of John Stands Out

The Gospels of Matthew, Mark, and Luke are called the *Synoptic Gospels*. This name is applied because these three books are noticeably similar, while the Gospel of John is quite different.[13] W. Hall Harris III, Professor of New Testament Studies at Dallas Theological Seminary says[14]:

"The synoptics are written from a third person point of view, describing the events as if the authors had personally observed all of them and were reporting what they saw at the time. Thus they are basically descriptive in their approach. John's Gospel, on the other hand, although also written from a third person point of view, is more reflective, clearly later than the events he describes. The author of the Fourth Gospel very carefully separates himself from the events he describes (cf. the role of the Beloved Disciple in the Fourth Gospel). However clear it is that he was an eyewitness of the life of Jesus, it is

15

no less clear that he looks back upon it from a temporal distance. While we see the events through his eyes, we are carefully guided to see the events of Jesus' life not as John saw them when they happened but as he now sees them. We understand more of the significance of the events described from the position the writer now holds than an eyewitness could have understood at the time the events took place. In this sense, John's Gospel is much more reflective."

The position of Professor Harris reveals to us why the Gospel of John is so important. It is providing a thoughtful presentation, rather than simply a recording of historical actions. For this reason, the Gospel of John stands out.

Instead of telling his version of events already spoken of in the Synoptic Gospels, the author of the Gospel of John writes about things the other writers didn't include. Approximately 92% of the Gospel of John is unique to that gospel.[15] The reason is expanded upon in an article in the Church of Jesus Christ of Latter-day Saints magazine called *New Era*:[16]

"John, or John the Beloved as he was known, served as one of the Apostles. His book was probably written last, as John seems to have already read the other Gospels before he wrote his own book. Often, instead of telling his version of an event or parable the others had already written about, he writes about things the other writers did not include. Also, John's Gospel includes the testimony of John the Baptist. It seems likely that he had some of the writings of John the Baptist.

John was writing to members of the Church, who already knew something of the Lord. John emphasizes Jesus's divine nature as the Son of God."

One of the most striking differences between the Gospel of John and the Synoptic Gospels is the presentation of Jesus as God in human form. The books of Matthew, Mark, and Luke present the human genealogy of Jesus. In the Gospel of John, he does not write about this, but instead, writes about the *Logos as form*. The Gospel of John (NIV) begins with:

In the beginning was the Word, and the Word was with God, and the Word was God. He was with God in the beginning. Through him all things were made; without him nothing was made that has been made. In him was life, and that life was the light of all mankind. The light shines in the darkness, and the darkness has not overcome it. (John 1:1-5)

In the first verses of the Gospel of John, the word "Word" comes from the original Greek "Logos", which is a term applied to Jesus Christ[17].

This is reinforced in verse 14:

The Word became flesh and made his dwelling among us. We have seen his glory, the glory of the one and only Son, who came from the Father, full of grace and truth.

This is again referred to in Revelation 19:13, where we find the description of "The Heavenly Warrior Defeats the Beast" (NIV):

He is dressed in a robe dipped in blood, and his name is the Word of God.

In John 1:15, we find the first quote of John the Baptist who was born before Christ, something you won't find in the Synoptic Gospels:

(John testified concerning him. He cried out, saying, "This is the one I spoke about when I said, 'He who comes after me has surpassed me because he was before me.'")

These assertions of Jesus being '*Logos in form*' in the opening chapter of John's Gospel are supported by other passages in the Gospel of John (4:26, 8:24, 8:28, 8:58, 10:30, and 13:19). This is also supported by Acts 20:28 (written by the author of the Gospel of Luke).

In John 1:1 we read, "*In the beginning was the Word, and the Word was with God, and the Word was God.*" In John 1:14 we read "*The Word became flesh and made his dwelling among us.*" This is confirmation of Jesus being God in the flesh. Yes, for some people, the concept of God and Jesus being the same person is hard to understand, but that concept is the basis of the Holy Trinity.

I believe there is ample evidence to support that the Gospel of John is authentic, reliable, and authoritative. The differences in John from the Synoptic Gospels should give us pause to be far more thoughtful and appreciative of what the author is presenting to us.

Reading the Gospel of John

Many people find the Gospel of John difficult to read. Not that it isn't understandable; rather, the wording and cadence of the passages are not what they are used to. If you find this is the case, try reading the passages out loud. Hearing the words you are reading can help with this.

When we read this book or any book in the Bible, we can't simply glean the words and leave it at that. We need to read the divinely inspired words with several lenses:

What was the time period it was written? To whom was it written? What is the subject of the surrounding passage, that is to say, what is the context of the passage you are reading in relation to the passages before it, after it, the whole chapter, and the whole book. We must apply both emotional intelligence and critical thinking to the words we read and how we understand them. Taking the time to do so, however, is a worthwhile and rewarding pursuit. Don't simply rely on the dogmatic interpretation of doctrinal agenda to give you the meaning of the word of the Lord, take it upon yourself to know the word of the Lord experientially.

Whenever I sit down to study passages, I always start with a prayer that God will help me understand the passages as he intended them to be understood.

"Ask, and it will be given you; seek, and you will find; knock, and it will be opened to you. For everyone who asks receives; the one who seeks finds; and to the one who knocks, the door will be opened." - Matthew 7:7-8

"If any of you lacks wisdom, you should ask God, who gives generously to all without finding fault, and it will be given to you." - James 1:5

There are many versions of the Bible. That is not to say these versions are different, they are not. They all say the same thing. However, they say it in slightly different ways. I grew up with the King James Version (KJV), and when I'm unclear on something in another version, I go back to the KJV. The Bible version I typically read and on which I base this work is the New International Version (NIV), as I find it easier to both read and understand — most of the time. Unless otherwise stated, quotations from the Bible used the New International Version (NIV).

When I find something that is of pivotal importance to my understanding, I refer to the original Koine Greek version for the New Testament. Luckily, you can find the original Greek translations on several websites (e.g. blueletterbible.org), and then pursue the meaning and context of the original language that was used. I have done this in the chapter you are reading, and I will do this several times throughout this book.

Ultimately, understanding the Bible rests with The Holy Spirit, which resides within you. Read your Bible carefully, critically, and with an open heart.

Ask God to guide you in your understanding of the Word and of His word. Come to know, understand, and love the word of God yourself, rather than relying solely on other's interpretations.

Chapter 2

John 3:16

"For God so loved the world that he gave his one and only Son, that whoever believes in him shall not perish but have eternal life."

This is probably the most well-known passage of the Bible, a passage that both Christian and non-Christian alike are familiar with. Unfortunately, the meaning of this verse gets lost by those of the far-left and the far-right who choose to use scripture for their own agenda.

The importance of God's love in this message is vital to understanding your relationship with God. To truly understand and know God's love is to remove hatred and intolerance from your heart. I hope that by the end of this chapter, your personal salvation will take on a new meaning and a new understanding, especially through the power of God's love.

The actions of Christian hate groups run contrary to the message that this well-known verse is preaching. If God loves, how can we not love? If

God does not hate, how can we hate? This takes me to the *Parable of Ten Thousand Talents* (also called the *Parable of the Unmerciful Servant*, or the *Parable of the Two Debtors*):

If God has forgiven us for so much (because none of us is without sin), how can we not forgive others for so little?

To fully understand John 3:16, we need to fully understand five key parts:

1. Whom "the world" refers to.
2. God's unconditional love.
3. The meaning of "belief."
4. The meaning of "perish."
5. The meaning of "eternal life."

The World

When the author of the Gospel of John related the words of Jesus Christ, they were written in Koine Greek. I will start by drawing your attention to the word "world" in John 3:16. In the original Greek text, the word was written as κόσμος (*kósmos*) - meaning world, people, cosmos, or universe.

The author had a choice of words to use if he solely meant the word in reference to the physical planet. The author could have used υφήλιος (*huphélios*) which means world or globe. The word could also have been written as σύμπαν (*sumpan*) meaning universe, cosmos, world, or macrocosm.

However, the author chose the word κόσμος (*kósmos)*, the only one of the three that includes "people" in its interpretation. This tells us that when Jesus said, "For God so loved the world ..." that he was saying, "For God so loved *all the people* of the world ..."

In a 2006 sermon, Pastor John Courson of Applegate Christian Fellowship explained that this phrase was how God, "Wants to gather together all things in Christ."

Dr. Charles Stanley, from In Touch Ministries, explains it like this[18]:

"That encompasses every single person who has ever been born, every single person that will be born, until the day that Jesus Christ comes again."

During the Sermon on the Mount, Jesus specifically addresses the idea of love for our enemies, or rather, love for those whom we are different from. In Matthew 5:43-48 we read:

"You have heard that it was said, 'Love your neighbor and hate your enemy.' But I tell you, love your enemies and pray for those who persecute you, that you may be children of your Father in heaven. He causes his sun to rise on the evil and the good, and sends rain on the righteous and the unrighteous. If you love those who love you, what reward will you get? Are not even the tax collectors doing that? And if you greet only your own people, what are you doing more than others? Do not even pagans do that? Be perfect, therefore, as your heavenly Father is perfect."

In this passage, Jesus is teaching us that treating anyone that we don't love or normally associate with, in a manner that is different from someone that we do love or associate with, is wrong. There's simply no getting around it. Hating anyone, even a sinner, is wrong for us. It is not what God/Jesus wants from us. It is not how we have been instructed to behave.

God's unconditional love

Chapter three of the Gospel of John opens with Jesus talking to Nicodemus. Nicodemus was a Pharisee, a member of the Jewish ruling council (Sanhedrin), and a teacher of Israel:

"He was early convinced that Christ came from God, but was not ready at once to rank himself among His followers. In John 3:1-20, he first appears as a timid inquirer after the truth, learning the great doctrines of regeneration and atonement. In John 7:45-52, we see him cautiously defending the Savior before the Sanhedrin. At last, in the trying scene of the crucifixion, he avowed himself a believer, and came with Joseph of Arimathea to pay the last duties to the body of Christ, which they took down from the cross, embalmed, and laid in the sepulchre, John 19:39." - ATS Bible Dictionary

Nicodemus met with Jesus at night, presumably so that he would not be seen with him. In verses one through fifteen, Jesus is responding to Nicodemus' questions regarding the meaning of being born again. Don Smith, former pastor at Christ Community Church in Laguna Hills, CA, said in a 2004 sermon that John 3:16 is a summation of Jesus' conversation with Nicodemus. Dr. Charles Stanley agreed with this by writing[19], "Then He gave a brief statement to summarize the plan of salvation."

As a summation, it is an extremely powerful statement. This verse reveals the immensity of God's love, manifested not just because he sent his

Son, but because he sent his Son to the world, to all people, to all the sinners and unbelievers.

What Jesus said to Nicodemus in John 3:16 is the ultimate argument against the legalism of other religions.

The word 'legalism' does not occur in the Bible. It is a term Christians use to describe a doctrinal position emphasizing a system of rules and regulations for achieving both salvation and spiritual growth. Legalists believe in and demand a strict literal adherence to rules and regulations. Doctrinally, it is a position essentially opposed to grace.[20]

Throughout the New Testament we learn of God's love for us. We learn of His desire that we love Him and His desire that we love one another. Jesus does not preach of God's intolerance, rather, he preaches of God's patience. God knows that it takes time to bring someone to uphold Jesus and accept salvation through faith. This understanding is inherent to The Great Commission of Matthew 28: 16-20:

"Then the eleven disciples went to Galilee, to the mountain where Jesus had told them to go. When they saw him, they worshiped him; but some doubted. Then Jesus came to them and said, "All authority in heaven and on earth has been given to

me. Therefore go and make disciples of all nations, baptizing them in the name of the Father and of the Son and of the Holy Spirit, and teaching them to obey everything I have commanded you. And surely I am with you always, to the very end of the age."

God knows that it will take time to make disciples of all nations (bring the word of God to others), and while that is happening, God still loves us — *without condition.*

In an undated radio broadcast by Dr. J. Vernon McGee, distributed by *Thru the Bible Radio Network* (ttb.org), he said of John 3:16 that:

God didn't save the world with His love, He saves by grace, the gift of God; but He so loved the world that whoever believed in Him would receive that grace, He didn't send Jesus to condemn the world, or to judge the world, He sent Him to save the world.

In a sermon, Charles Spurgeon addresses God's love for a world that is filled with those who do not love him:[21]

Tonight, we have to talk about the love of God: "God so loved the world." That love of God is a very wonderful thing, especially when we see it set upon a lost, ruined, guilty world. What was there in

29

the world that God should love it? There was nothing lovable in it. No fragrant flower grew in that arid desert. Enmity to him, hatred to his truth, disregard of his law, rebellion against his commandments; those were the thorns and briars which covered the waste land; but no desirable thing blossomed there. Yet, "God loved the world," says the text; "so" loved it, that even the writer of the book of John could not tell us how much; but so greatly, so divinely, did he love it that he gave his Son, his only Son, to redeem the world from perishing, and to gather out of it a people to his praise.

Whence came that love? Not from anything outside of God himself. God's love springs from himself. He loves because it is his nature to do so. "God is love." As I have said already, nothing upon the face of the earth could have merited his love, though there was much to merit his displeasure. This stream of love flows from its own secret source in the eternal Deity, and it owes nothing to any earth-born rain or rivulet; it springs from beneath the everlasting throne, and fills itself full from the springs of the infinite. God loved because he would love. When we enquire why the Lord loved this man sor that, we have to come back to our Saviour's answer to the question, "Even so, Father, for so it seemed good in thy sight." **God has such love in**

his nature that he must needs *(sic)* **let it flow forth to a world perishing by its own wilful sin; and when it flowed forth it was so deep, so wide, so strong, that even inspiration could not compute its measure, and therefore the Holy Spirit gave us that great little word SO, and left us to attempt the measurement, according as we perceive more and more of love divine.**

(Author's note: the bold is mine.)

The Bible makes it very clear that God wants us to turn away from sin, that He wants us to be faithful, and that He wants us to accept the salvation purchased with His Son's blood, He wants us to be good to each other and to love one another. What the Bible also makes very clear, is that His love for you is not conditional upon these things.

Now I'll pose a question: If God loves this person, or that person, so much that he let his Son die on the cross, how can you love that person any less? God loves every single person in the world, "For God so *loved* the *world*". He *loves* everyone, including those who have sinned.

I've had the argument put to me that the Bible tells us to rebuke sinners. Indeed, it does — but in a specific context.

If your brother or sister sins, go and point out their fault, just between the two of you. If they listen to you, you have won them over. But if they will not listen, take one or two others along, so that 'every matter may be established by the testimony of two or three witnesses.' If they still refuse to listen, tell it to the church; and if they refuse to listen even to the church, treat them as you would a pagan or a tax collector. (Matthew 18:15-17)

This passage from Matthew 18 is dealing specifically with sin within the church. It tells us how to look after one another in the church when someone gives in to sin or strays from the narrow gate. This is not about public shaming.

As for those who persist in sin, rebuke them in the presence of all, so that the rest may stand in fear. (1 Timothy 5:20 - ESV)

Some who would argue for public demonstrations against sinners use the above passage from First Timothy. Again, though, this passage is specifically about the church body. The same verse in the NIV is written:

But those elders who are sinning you are to reprove before everyone, so that the others may take warning. (1 Timothy 5:20 - NIV)

This verse gains context, however, when you look at the preceding passages:

The elders who direct the affairs of the church well are worthy of double honor, especially those whose work is preaching and teaching. For Scripture says, "Do not muzzle an ox while it is treading out the grain," and "The worker deserves his wages." Do not entertain an accusation against an elder unless it is brought by two or three witnesses. But those elders who are sinning you are to reprove before everyone, so that the others may take warning. (1 Timothy 5:17-20)

In verse 20, the term "everyone" refers to everyone in the church. To argue that the world is the church would be inconsistent with the audience of First Timothy. This book is the first of the Pastoral Epistles (i.e. 1 Timothy, 2 Timothy, Titus). It was written "to a young pastor named Timothy working in the church at Ephesus."[22]

Again, Luke 17:3 provides a focused understanding about rebuking:

So watch yourselves. If your brother or sister sins against you, rebuke them; and if they repent, forgive them. (Luke 17:3 - NIV)

Pastor Chuck Smith has this to say on the verse in an undated sermon[23]:

"The Bible tells us that we should reprove, that we should rebuke. And if he repents forgive him. So your brother trespass against you, rebuke him, and say, "Hey, that isn't right, you shouldn't have done that." "Oh, I'm sorry. Forgive me?" "Yes, I forgive you." Should be just like that."

An important point to note here is that in Luke 17, the author is talking specifically about interpersonal sins,[24,25] though more specifically, it is about one who causes another to stumble, as is 1 Timothy 5:20.

David Guzik's study guide explains that Luke 17:3 is about one-on-one sin[26]:

a. If your brother sins against you, rebuke him: When someone sins against you, you should not pretend that it never happened. You need to rebuke that brother in love.

i. Love is the rule here; we obviously can't walk around keep a record of every little offense committed against us. One aspect of the fruit of the Spirit is longsuffering (Galatians 5:22), and we need to be able to suffer long with the slights and petty offences that come our way in daily living.

Ephesians 4:2 says that we should love with longsuffering, bearing with one another in love. Don't be too sensitive; bear with one another.

ii. But in love, when we are sinned against in a significant way, we must follow Ephesians 4:15 as the pattern: we need to speak the truth in love. Love isn't going to other people about it; love isn't bottling it up inside of you. Love is getting it straight with the person who sinned against you.

As I have said, we get a better understanding through context. This idea of sin and rebuke from this passage is better understood by reading Guzik's commentary on verse 1 and 2 of the same chapter (same citation):

1. (Luke 17:1-2) The danger of stumbling another.

Then He said to the disciples, "It is impossible that no offenses should come, but woe to him through whom they do come! It would be better for him if a millstone were hung around his neck, and he were thrown into the sea, than that he should offend one of these little ones."

a. Jesus, through the account of Lazarus and the rich man, has made it clear that eternity is for real, and no one from beyond will come back to warn us. It is all the more imperative how we live and show Jesus to others on this side of eternity, because right now counts forever.

b. It is impossible: It is inevitable that people be offended, but woe to the person through whom those offenses come. What does Jesus mean when He speaks of offenses?

i. The Greek word used here is *skandalon*, and it comes from the word for a bent-stick-the stick that springs the trap or sets the bait. It also was used for a stumbling block, something that people trip over.

ii. In the Bible, sometimes a *skandalon* is good-such as the way that people "trip" over Jesus, and are offended at the gospel (Romans 9:33, 1 Corinthians 1:23, Galatians 5:11).

iii. But among brothers in Jesus, a *skandalon* is bad. It can be false counsel (Matthew 16:23), and it can be leading a brother into sin by your "liberty" (Romans 14:13). Division and false teaching brings a *skandalon* among God's people (Romans 16:17).

c. Woe to him through whom they do come: Essentially, Jesus is saying: "People are going to take the bait-but woe to you if you offer the hook. People are going to trip up-but woe to you if you set the stumbling block in their way."

i. It would better for such a one to die a horrible death, such as having a millstone hung around your neck and being thrown into the sea.

ii. This is a lesson that the church learned the hard way in trying to help God to curse the Jewish race for their rejection of the Messiah; the curse came back on the church worse than ever. If someone seems ripe for the judgment or discipline of God, let God do it. Get out of the way. God doesn't need you as an instrument of His judgment, only as an instrument of His love

d. 1 John 2:10 explains the solution to being a *skandalon* to others-love: He who loves his brother abides in the light, and there is no cause for stumbling in him. If we love our brother, we will not bring an offense into their life.

The point of the above, if it isn't already clear, is that "rebuke" is about one-on-one sin or offence. It is not about marching in the streets and shouting hateful things. It is not our place to take public action against someone because we don't think they are returning God's love:

Accept him whose faith is weak, without passing judgment on disputable matters - Romans 14:1

But love your enemies, and do good, and lend, expecting nothing in return; and your reward will be great, and you will be sons of the Most High; **for He Himself is kind to ungrateful and evil men.** *Luke 6:35*

(Authors Note: The bold is mine.)

John 3:16 teaches us that salvation comes from faith, not from completing *pro forma* acts according to doctrine. Additionally, the verse of John 3:16 reveals that this was done because God loves us, not because we love God. In 1 John 4:9-10, we read:

This is how God showed his love among us: He sent his one and only Son into the world that we might live through him. This is love: not that we loved God, but that he loved us and sent his Son as an atoning sacrifice for our sins.

Romans 5:6-8, written by the Apostle Paul, reinforce the writings of 1 John:

You see, at just the right time, when we were still powerless, Christ died for the ungodly. Very rarely will anyone die for a righteous person, though for a good person someone might possibly dare to die. But God demonstrates his own love for us in this: While we were still sinners, Christ died for us.

The verse from 1 John and Romans helps us understand what it is that Jesus is saying to Nicodemus. God knows that the world is filled with sinners and unbelievers. God sends his son for those sinners, so that they may be redeemed by grace, redeemed by God's own unconditional love. God sent his Son to die for those sinners, *while they were still sinners.*

If we turn to Luke 10:25-28, the beginning of *The Parable of the Good Samaritan* helps us understand John 3:16:

On one occasion an expert in the law stood up to test Jesus. "Teacher," he asked, "what must I do to inherit eternal life?"

"What is written in the Law?" he replied. "How do you read it?"

He answered, "'Love the Lord your God with all your heart and with all your soul and with all your strength and with all your mind'; and, 'Love your neighbor as yourself.'"

"You have answered correctly," Jesus replied. "Do this and you will live."

For many people, Luke 10:25-28 is very confusing. How is it that we get salvation by accepting Jesus as our saviour, but we must also "do" something? This is because of the depth of the text of the Bible, versus the proper instruction of the passage.

Belief

To understand how *The Parable of the Good Samaritan* (Luke 10:25-28) affects the interpretation of John 3:16, we have to consider John 14:6, which reads:

> *I am the way and the truth and the life. No one comes to the Father except through me.*

The setting for John 14 was just before the Passover Festival (John 13:1). It was during a gathering that later became known as the Last Supper. On this day, the apostles were aware that Jesus was going to be taken and crucified (John 12:20-36). Jesus takes to comforting the disciples with his words and the promise of a place for them in heaven. This chapter also reveals the promise of the Holy Spirit (John 13:15-27) which is finally given to man in Acts 2:1-12.

The passage begins with Jesus telling his disciples to not be upset, but to believe in Him as they believe in God. He reiterates that He is going to prepare a place for them in His Father's house. He tells them that they know the way to the place He is going.

The Apostle Thomas (later to become known as Doubting Thomas) then asks in John 14:5, "Lord, we don't know where you are going, so how can we know the way?"

Jesus responds in verse 6:

I am the way and the truth and the life. No one comes to the Father except through me.

Again, as in John 3:16, we find Jesus making a summation. If we look back to John 6:29, we find Jesus is talking to some of the crowd of 5,000 that he fed (John 6:1-14). He is speaking to people who grew up in the Hebrew faith, in a very legalistic tradition. He challenges them on the reason they are seeking Him, telling them to seek Him out for the salvation He offers in the eternal life, rather than what He can provide them in the here and now.

The crowd then asks Him, "What must we do to do the works God requires?" (John 6:28). In this question, we see that what Jesus has said to them was lost on them. They are still in the mindset of a legalistic form of worship, a legalistic pursuit of entry to heaven. Jesus responds to them with a very simple answer in verse 29:

Jesus answered, "The work of God is this: to believe in the one he has sent."

The original author used the Greek word: πιστεύω *(pisteuō)* which I will examine in depth a bit further on. For now, I'll explain that it means more than just believing, it conveys the idea of yielding or surrendering.

We see in this verse that Jesus is reiterating that entry to heaven comes from faith, but it is a faith that is deeper and richer than you may have previously understood that word to mean. By completely surrendering or yielding to Christ, we become one with him, that is, we follow the way He lives His life and live our lives in the same manner.

With this answer, we see that entry to heaven comes from what is in the heart, not the outward face that you show the world. Still, though, Jesus is fighting an uphill battle, even after all that He has done and taught in His adult life. In John 6:25-59 we read His discourse on the Bread of Life, again presenting the faith-based approach to eternal life. Yet immediately, in John 6:60-71, all but the twelve apostles desert Him.

In John 8:12, Jesus again offers His example as the path to eternal life:

When Jesus spoke again to the people, he said, "I am the light of the world. Whoever follows me will never walk in darkness, but will have the light of life."

Again, Jesus is telling us to follow His example, not simply profess that we accept Him and believe (modernistic interpretation) in Him.

Taking that Jesus wants us to follow His example and that He confirms to a lawmaker that one must love God, and love one another, then we have a clear indication of the totality and scope of God's unconditional love. That is, love without condition for who or what you are, whether you believe or not, whether you are a sinner or not.

In the passage of Luke 10:25-28, some may wonder if in fact Jesus is declaring requirements for salvation (legalism), where He has before preached that salvation comes from faith. In a discourse on this passage, Eng Hoe Lim, author of *The Gospel of the Kingdom: Revealing the Heart of God*, was asked by a man[27]:

"To be honest, I must admit that I do not love my neighbor as myself. If what you say is true, then that means I am not saved. What you are telling me is that I still need to earn my salvation with good works, and so, as soon as this seminar ends, I need

43

to rush out and go and love someone to make sure I am saved. You are confusing us. You are taking us back to the law."

In the New Testament, Jesus is often talking with Hebrews. In John 3:16, He is talking to Nicodemus, a Pharisee; in Luke 10:25-28, He is also talking to a Hebrew. While Jesus is reinforcing His message to a Hebrew, this passage in Luke is for everyone: Hebrews, Gentiles, unbelievers, *and* followers of Christ. This passage is as true and valid today, as it was 2,000-plus years ago.

There is no inconsistency between John 3:16 and Luke 10:25-28. In the John 3:16 verse, we are also being told to do good works.

"In Jn.3:16 the word "believe" in the original Greek, is "pisteuo". "Pisteuo" is not about a change of belief. "Pisteuo" is not just a mental assent and acceptance of something to be true. "Pisteuo" is a total trust and abandonment of oneself upon the object of the belief. There is no English word that is equivalent in meaning to the word "pisteuo". The closest word that the translators could find for the word "pisteuo" is "believe". So they translated "pisteuo" as "believe". But the word "believe" on its own does not convey what "pisteuo" actually means. "Pisteuo" describes an action that is like sitting on a chair – you put your entire weight on the chair. You abandon yourself and rest totally on the chair – in complete trust. "Pisteuo" also conveys the idea of yielding or surrendering. The word "faith", in the original Greek, is "pistis", the noun of "pisteuo", and means the same thing."[28]

The story of the French tightrope walker, Charles Blondin, crossing Niagara Falls illustrates what true faith is; what truly believing in Jesus means[29]:

In June of 1859 he attempted to become the first person to cross a tightrope stretched over a quarter of a mile across the mighty Niagara Falls.

He walked across 160 feet above falls several times, each time with a different daring feat - once in a sack, on stilts, on a bicycle, in the dark, and once he even carried a stove and cooked an omelet! On one occasion though, he asked for the participation of a volunteer. A large crowd gathered and a buzz of excitement ran along both sides of the river bank. The crowd "Oooohed!" and "Aaaaahed!" as Blondin carefully walked across one dangerous step after another -- blindfolded and pushing a wheelbarrow.

Upon reaching the other side, the crowd's applause was louder than the roar of the falls! Blondin suddenly stopped and addressed his audience: "Do you believe I can carry a person across in this wheelbarrow?" The crowd enthusiastically shouted, "Yes, yes, yes. You are the greatest tightrope walker in the world. You can do anything!"

"Okay," said Blondin, "Get in the wheelbarrow....."

No-one did!

The story of Charles Blondin paints a real life picture of what faith actually is. The crowd had watched his daring feats. They said they believed, but their actions proved they truly didn't.

When we read "... *that whoever believes in Him ...*" we are being told to not only profess our faith, but to put all of our trust in Jesus. We must surrender our lives to Jesus; He has to be the Lord of all. It's not enough to just 'believe' as we understand the word; we must make every part of our life reflective of that absolute faith. To surrender so completely, to become "one" with Jesus, then our hearts and our actions will reflect what He teaches us — *what He is*.

In 1 John 4:7-8 we read:

Dear friends, let us love one another, for love comes from God. Everyone who loves has been born of God and knows God. Whoever does not love does not know God, because God is love.

Just a few verses later, in 1 John 4:11-13 we read:

Dear friends, since God so loved us, we also ought to love one another. No one has ever seen God; but if we love one another, God lives in us and his love is made complete in us. This is how we know that we live in him and he in us: He has given us of his Spirit.

So, the Bible is making it very clear to us: to believe in Jesus means that we must follow His example. If we love God, if we love Jesus, then we will love our fellow man. We won't do so because we must, and we won't do it simply to please the Lord. The effect of God's love, Jesus example, and the presence of the Holy Spirit will change our nature in a way that loving our fellow man will simply be who we are.

"Love is not just a feeling. Love is doing. And love is a choice. Often love compels us to make choices to do what is right and necessary against how we feel – especially when we choose to love our enemies ... or just a horrible neighbor! Jesus said, "If you love Me, keep my commands" (Jn.14:15). There is no "love" button on us that God is going to press from time to time to get us to love. We have to love. We have to choose to love despite the sin nature in us pulling us in the other direction. If we don't, because we refuse to yield and surrender ourselves to Him as Lord, then that's not "pisteuo", no matter how much you are trusting in Jesus for salvation, and if we do not "pisteuo" in Jesus, then we are certainly not one with God, meaning we do not have eternal life."[30]

Perish

But if we don't follow Jesus' example of love for our fellow man, there is a risk, a price. In John 3:16, we read the word "perish" with the understanding of death. However, the original Greek word ἀπόλλυμι *(apollymi)* has a meaning that is deeper than simply physical death. HELPS™ Word-studies tell us about this word[31]:

622 apóllymi (from 575 /apó, "away from," which intensifies ollymi, "to destroy") – properly, fully destroy, cutting off entirely (note the force of the prefix, 575 /apó).

622 /apóllymi ("violently/completely perish") implies permanent (absolute) destruction, i.e. to cancel out (remove); "to die, with the implication of ruin and destruction" (L & N, 1, 23.106); cause to be lost (utterly perish) by experiencing a miserable end.

[This is also the meaning of 622 /apóllymi dating back to Homer (900 bc.)]

48

The *NAS Exhaustive Concordance of the Bible with Hebrew-Aramaic and Greek Dictionaries* gives an interesting word count for the various interpretations of this word:

bring (1), destroy (17), destroyed (9), dying (1), end (1), killed (1), lose (10), loses (7), lost (14), passed away (1), perish (14), perishable (1), perished (4), perishes (1), perishing (6), put to death (1), ruined (3).

We find that this word interpreted as "perish" in the verse is translated in reference to death and dying 34 times, whereas it is interpreted as destruction or loss 57 times. This leads us to understand that in the context of this verse, *perish* isn't about death, it is about suffering the absence of everything wonderful that comes from our faith in, and our love for Jesus.

Paul Kroll, a journalist who worked for Grace Communion International, writes that in this verse, "perish" and "eternal life" are presented as opposites[32]. He further says:

The Bible does not define "perish." Some verses support the concept of complete destruction, or annihilation; other verses support the concept of eternal conscious suffering. Interpreters of both persuasions agree, however, following the biblical use of the term, that the unrepentant will perish in the lake of fire.

We cannot assume that "perish" means that consciousness will cease. The Bible speaks of unbelievers as being dead (Ephesians 2:1; John 5:24), yet they are certainly conscious! Since the Bible uses the word "dead" in such a metaphorical way, it may also use the word "perish" in a metaphorical way, especially when it is talking about the age to come, an afterlife, of which we have no experience.

In the book of Revelation, we find references to the "lake of fire and Sulphur" (20:10, 21:8, 20:14-15, et al.). It should not be lost on us that the eternal suffering is formed with the imagery of a *lake of fire*, which is in counterpoint to Jesus offering his promise of salvation as the *water of life*. This offers us further insight that to *perish*, is to suffer a life absent of Jesus' presence and promise.

Bill Randles, pastor at a non-denominational Pentecostal church in Marion, Iowa, explains the concept of "perish" very succinctly[33]:

The new birth that Jesus offers, interrupts the process of destruction, it reverses the disintegration of the soul, by the impartation of eternal life, which is the gift of the very Life of God. Remember that the discussion of John 3 is the new birth, being "born from above". If there is both a physical and spiritual birth, does it not follow that there is a physical and spiritual death?

As the slogan I once saw put it so well, "If you are only born once, you are going to die twice, but if you are born twice, you will only die once!

Dr. Audrey Drummonds of the Interior Coverings Ministry says this[34]:

The Spirit if God is using the word "perish" for us to understand the paths of life, the options that are taken, and the consequences that occur. We lose the ability to appropriate the fullness of our inheritance with our relationship with God as Father when we don't stay focused on Him.

In John 3:16, "perish" is not about the physical death. Rather, it is about the lack of spiritual life here and now, and the lack of an after-life in heaven. Those who do not accept God and follow the example set by Jesus will live a life on earth that is devoid of the grace, love, and joy that is enjoyed by those who do accept the wonderful gift that God is offering us.

Eternal or everlasting life

The final part of this misunderstood verse that we need to examine is "eternal life" (NIV) or "everlasting life" (KJV).

Most people who read this verse read it as *eternal life in heaven after I die*. While this is part of that assurance, the term eternal/everlasting life comes from the original Greek text: αἰώνιος *(aiōnios)*. Referring to HELPS™ Word-studies, our understanding of this simple term is going to be pleasantly, if not surprisingly, altered[35]:

Cognate: 166 aiṓnios (an adjective, derived from 165 /aiṓn ("an age, having a particular character and quality") – properly, "age-like" ("like-an-age"), i.e. an "age-characteristic" (the quality describing a particular age); (figuratively) the unique quality (reality) of God's life at work in the believer, i.e. as the Lord manifests His self-existent life (as it is in His sinless abode of heaven). "Eternal (166 /aiṓnios) life operates simultaneously outside of time, inside of time, and beyond time – i.e. what gives time its everlasting meaning for the believer through faith, yet is also time-independent. See 165 (aiōn).

[166 (aiṓnios) does not focus on the future per se, but rather on the quality of the age (165 /aiṓn) it relates to. Thus believers live in "eternal (166 /aiōnios) life" right now, experiencing this quality of God's life now as a present possession. (Note the Gk present tense of having eternal life in Jn 3:36, 5:24, 6:47; cf. Ro 6:23.)]

It is clear that what the original author of this verse wrote doesn't convey to readers of this day and age the depth of the meaning. The eternal/everlasting life that we are promised is not a pie-in-the-sky objective for the future. The eternal/everlasting life that we seek is right here, right now, and immediately upon us. The promise of God through Jesus is available to you *right now*.

Armed with our new understanding of John 3:16, perhaps we can read it this way:

For God so loved every single person in the word, even the sinners, that whosoever follows the example of love set by Jesus, shall not be given over to misery and destruction now and forever, but will enjoy the grace and joy of God's love and the transformative power of the Holy Spirit right now, *and* for eternity.

When I learned to understand scripture based on the original Koine Greek, my understanding of scripture changed. I gained a rich and deeper understanding of the "good news" by taking the time to understand it with a critical-thinking approach.

Unfortunately, much of the world doesn't receive the deeper understanding from careful study. Even more unfortunate, is that the most well-known verse in the Bible is thrown out to the world with little or no explanation. This verse is powerful, it is redemptive, and it presents a summation of God's attempt to bring the world to an understanding of how to live their lives. But when this verse is presented as a stand-alone verse, without proper exegesis (critical explanation or interpretation), it presents a confusing message.

With this new understanding of this verse, the question that comes foremost to my mind is: *Why are parts of Christianity such a warzone of competing ideologies and intolerance towards others?*

Why do Christians think that they can operate with anything *but* love for their fellow man, be they Christian, Jew, Muslim, sinner, believer, homosexual, polytheist, atheist, criminal, or saint?

To borrow a line[36] from the Jamie Kennedy character in *Malibu's Most Wanted*:

Don't be hatin'!

Chapter 3

John 14:6

Jesus answered, "I am the way and the truth and the life. No one comes to the Father except through me."

It's impossible to fully discuss or understand John 3:16 without examining John 14:6. As I said previously, this verse supports John 3:16. This is Jesus' expansion of the word "believes" and the depth of its meaning.

I find it heartbreaking that so many Christians simply *don't get it*.

The summation

The setting for John 14 was just before the Passover Festival (John 13:1). It was during a gathering that later became known as the *Last Supper*. On this day, the apostles were aware that Jesus was going to be taken and crucified (John 12:20-36). Jesus takes to comforting the disciples with his words and the promise of a place for them in heaven. This chapter also reveals the promise of the Holy Spirit (John 13:15-27) which is finally given to man in Acts 2:1-12.

The passage begins with Jesus telling his disciples to not be upset, but to believe in Him as they believe in God. He reiterates that He is going to prepare a place for them in His Father's house. He tells them that they know the way to the place He is going.

The Apostle Thomas then asks in John 14:5, "Lord, we don't know where you are going, so how can we know the way?"

Jesus responds:

I am the way and the truth and the life. No one comes to the Father except through me.

Again, as in John 3:16, we find Jesus making a summation. If we look back to John 6:29, we find Jesus is talking to some of the crowd of 5,000 that he fed (John 6:1-14). He is speaking to people who grew up in the Hebrew faith, in a very legalistic tradition. He challenges them on the reason they are seeking Him, telling them to seek Him out for the salvation He offers through the eternal/everlasting life, rather than what He can physically provide them in the here and now.

The crowd then asks Him, "What must we do to do the works God requires?" (John 6:28). In this question, we see that what Jesus has said to them was lost on them. They are still in the mindset of a legalistic form of worship, a legalistic pursuit of entry to heaven. Jesus responds to them with a very simple answer in verse 29:

Jesus answered, "The work of God is this: to believe in the one he has sent."

We see in this verse that Jesus is reiterating that entry to heaven comes from faith, not by the fulfillment of legalistic requirements, not by fulfilling items on a checklist like they have been used to. What He is saying is, "Follow My example."

Follow His example

With the answer to the crowd in John 6:29, we see that entry to heaven comes from following Jesus; from what is in the heart, not the outward face that you show the world. Still, though, Jesus is fighting an uphill battle, even after all that He has done and taught in His adult life. In John 6:25-59 we read His discourse on the Bread of Life, again presenting the faith-based approach to eternal life.

Yet immediately, in John 6:60-71, all but the twelve apostles desert him.

In John 8:12, Jesus again offers his example as the path to eternal life:

When Jesus spoke again to the people, he said, "I am the light of the world. Whoever follows me will never walk in darkness, but will have the light of life."

The original Greek text for John 8:12 uses the word φῶς (phōs) which translates as "the Light". Strong's Concordance Greek translation of the word says this means[37]: luminousness (in the widest application, natural or artificial, abstract or concrete, literal or figurative):—fire, light.

The same reference expands on this by quoting Thayer's Concordance to give the metaphorical meanings of:

2a) God is light because light has the extremely delicate, subtle, pure, brilliant quality

2b) of truth and its knowledge, together with the spiritual purity associated with it

2c) that which is exposed to the view of all, openly, publicly

2d) reason, mind

2d1) the power of understanding esp. moral and spiritual truth

The Greek word used for "he who follows" is ἀκολουθέω *(akoloutheō),* which Strong's defines as:[38] properly, to be in the same way with, i.e. to accompany (specially, as a disciple).

The Greek word used for "walk" is περιπατέω (peripatéō), which Strong's defines as:[39] to tread all around, i.e. walk at large (especially as proof of ability); figuratively, to live, deport oneself, follow (as a companion or votary).

The Greek word used for "the darkness" is σκοτία *(scotia),* which Strong's defines as: shadiness, i.e. obscurity (literally or figuratively).

This passage is once again Jesus' way of telling those who follow Him to behave in the same way that He does so that they are not lost to an unwelcome way of living that would cause them to be lost to what they seek.

In John 8:31-47, Jesus challenges the disbelievers by telling them they are not following the example of their proclaimed father, Abraham, but rather, they are following the example of the Devil:

To the Jews who had believed him, Jesus said, "If you hold to my teaching, you are really my disciples. Then you will know the truth, and the truth will set you free."

They answered him, "We are Abraham's descendants and have never been slaves of anyone. How can you say that we shall be set free?"

Jesus replied, "Very truly I tell you, everyone who sins is a slave to sin. Now a slave has no permanent place in the family, but a son belongs to it forever. So if the Son sets you free, you will be free indeed. I know that you are Abraham's descendants. Yet you are looking for a way to kill me, because you have no room for my word. I am telling you what I have seen in the Father's presence, and you are doing what you have heard from your father."

"Abraham is our father," they answered.

"If you were Abraham's children," said Jesus, "then you would do what Abraham did. As it is, you are looking for a way to kill me, a man who has told you the truth that I heard from God. Abraham did not do such things. You are doing the works of your own father."

"We are not illegitimate children," they protested. "The only Father we have is God himself."

Jesus said to them, "If God were your Father, you would love me, for I have come here from God. I have not come on my own; God sent me. Why is my language not clear to you? Because you are unable to hear what I say. You belong to your father, the devil, and you want to carry out your father's desires. He was a murderer from the beginning, not holding to the truth, for there is no truth in him. When he lies, he speaks his native language, for he is a liar and the father of lies. Yet because I tell the truth, you do not believe me! Can any of you prove me guilty of sin? If I am telling the truth, why don't you believe me? Whoever belongs to God hears what God says. The reason you do not hear is that you do not belong to God."

To understand the contention in John 8:31-47, you need to understand God's relationship with Abraham.

In Acts 3:13, Peter is speaking to a group of Israelites who just witnessed him healing a lame beggar. The people were surprised and looking at them as though their own power or godliness had made the man walk (Acts 3:12). His response to them was:

"The God of Abraham, Isaac and Jacob, the God of our fathers, has glorified his servant Jesus." (Acts 3:13)

Abraham was the first of the three patriarchs of Judaism. He also plays a prominent role in Judaism, Christianity, and Islam (the Abrahamic religions). Abraham was the first man on earth that God appeared to (Genesis 12:7-9, Genesis 17:1, Genesis 18:1, Genesis 22:11-14).

God called Abraham *His friend*. In James 2:23 we read:

And the scripture was fulfilled that says, "Abraham believed God, and it was credited to him as righteousness," and he was called God's friend.

In that verse, James was quoting from Isaiah 41:8:

"But you, Israel, my servant, Jacob, whom I have chosen, you descendants of Abraham my friend …"

Abraham, who almost sacrificed his son Isaac, is one of the most important people in the Pentateuch (the first five books of the Old Testament). We can see that Jesus referring to the descendants of Abraham as following the Devil would have been a shocking and truly noteworthy statement.

So, why did He do this?

There are people who consider this passage to be an anti-Jewish sentiment, which it most clearly is not. Jesus is not making a proclamation that covers all the Hebrews or all the descendants of Abraham. Jesus is talking to a very particular group of descendants of Abraham. In John 8, He is talking to a group of people that want to kill Him. In John 8:37 we read:

I know that you are Abraham's descendants. Yet you are looking for a way to kill me, because you have no room for my word.

In the next verse, Jesus is saying that what they are doing according to their desire, what they have heard from their father, is not what Jesus has been teaching:

I am telling you what I have seen in the Father's presence, and you are doing what you have heard from your father."

Note the differences in the spelling of "father". Jesus is telling them what He has seen in the "Father's" presence; capital "F", meaning God. He is then saying they are doing what they heard from their "father"; small "f", meaning a human father who is neither God nor Abraham.

When the group protests that Abraham, God's friend, is their father, Jesus responds:

"If you were Abraham's children," said Jesus, "then you would do what Abraham did. As it is, you

are looking for a way to kill me, a man who has told you the truth that I heard from God. Abraham did not do such things. You are doing the works of your own father."

This is where He is making the distinction that this group may be born of Abraham, but they are not behaving as Abraham would have had them behave.

The hidden point of this discourse in John 8 is about descendants following the example set by their father. As Jesus pointed out that this group is not following the example of Abraham, Jesus is also highlighting the fact that He is following the example of His Father: love one another.

By the time we get to John 14, we can see that Jesus has been dealing with a lot of disbelief and outright aggression. Regardless of all His good works, His teachings, His example, and His words, he is still being challenged by the twelve closest to him.

So, what does John 14:6 truly mean?

I am the way and the truth and the life. No one comes to the Father except through me.

This summation is Jesus' way of telling the disciples to behave as He has, to follow His example. He has spent His adult life setting an example of forgiveness, of brotherly love, and of tolerance. Jesus ate with sinners, He mingled with believers and unbelievers, and He did not judge, because judgement is the purview of God.

Chapter 4

Conclusion

I am not seeking glory for myself; but there is one who seeks it, and he is the judge. (John 8:50)

The message from John 3:16 and John 14:6 is consistent and simple:

- Love everyone as God loves them.
- Claim your reward now and ever after by following His example.
- Love, tolerance, compassion, good works, and sacrifice are the way to heaven — *not because you have to, but because following Jesus compels you to want to reshape yourself, your nature, in* His *image.*

When we believe in Jesus, when we follow Jesus, we are following the example that He sets for us. In doing so, we do not judge, we do not point fingers, we do not engage in hateful speech or reproach, we do not condemn.

Judge not, and you will not be judged; condemn not, and you will not be condemned; forgive, and you will be forgiven; (Luke 6:37)

The misunderstandings of John 3:16 and John 14:6 are evident in the amount of hatred, vitriol, condemnation, and judgement coming from Christian sources.

There is only one Lawgiver and Judge, the one who is able to save and destroy. But you--who are you to judge your neighbor? (James 4:12)

Pope Francis said[40]:

"No one must use the name of God to commit violence," the spiritual leader of the world's 1.2 billion Catholics said at the Catholic University. "To kill in the name of God is a grave sacrilege. To discriminate in the name of God is inhuman."

"Let no one consider themselves to be the 'armor' of God while planning and carrying out acts of violence and oppression," the pontiff told officials at the presidential palace in Tirana.

In May 2009, Scott Roeder shot Dr. George Tiller, using his contradictory Christian beliefs as justification for the murder[41]. In 2014, Larry McQuilliams fired over 100 shots at a police station, courthouse, and a Mexican consulate[42]. In his vehicle, officials found a copy of *Vigilantes of Christendom*. Writings found in his apartment indicated that he considered himself a "high priest".

Judge not, that you be not judged. For with the judgment you pronounce you will be judged, and with the measure you use it will be measured to you. Why do you see the speck that is in your brother's eye, but do not notice the log that is in your own eye? Or how can you say to your brother, 'Let me take the speck out of your eye,' when there is the log in your own eye? You hypocrite, first take the log out of your own eye, and then you will see clearly to take the speck out of your brother's eye. (Matthew 7:1-5)

I can't even begin to list the Westboro Baptist Church examples, nor all the other churches/religious groups that protest over gay or transgender people.

Sin in context

Let's have a look at the Ten Commandments. How many Christians have ever taken the Lord's name in vain? How many have ever worked on a Sunday? How many have always done every single thing that their mother or father told them to? How many have ever said a mean-spirited thing about their parents? How many have committed adultery, or been divorced? How many Christian men realise that in divorcing their wife, they are causing their wife to commit adultery according to the Bible?

Therefore you have no excuse, O man, every one of you who judges. For in passing judgment on another you condemn yourself, because you, the judge, practice the very same things. (Romans 2:1)

How many Christians have had moments of intense pride for how much better they are than someone else for something they accomplished? Yep, God detests that (Proverbs 16:5).

Do you often get so drunk you aren't in control of yourself? Doesn't matter if you did anything bad or not, Galatians 5:21 says that those who live like this will not inherit the kingdom of God.

Have you ever been jealous of someone or something and not been able to get over it? Have you ever gone into a fit of rage about someone or something? Yes, read Galatians chapter 5, might as well get the whole picture.

Have you ever loaned someone money and charged interest for it? Have you ever failed to pay back money or a tool that you borrowed? Read Ezekiel 18:5-17.

Referring to those who cheat at commerce, Deuteronomy 25:16 says, "*...For the Lord your*

God detests anyone who does these things, anyone who deals dishonestly." If that isn't potent enough for you, here is the King James Version of the verse, *"For all that do such things, and all that do unrighteously, are an abomination unto the Lord thy God."*

Is that enough? Do I need to go on? Yes, I think I do.

In Proverbs 6:16-19 we learned that there are six things the Lord (God) hates, and seven that are detestable to him:

- haughty eyes (arrogance)
- a lying tongue
- hands that shed innocent blood (gossip, emotional abuse, physical assault, or murder)
- a heart that devises wicked schemes
- feet that are quick to rush into evil,
- a false witness who pours out lies
- a person who stirs up conflict in the community

Personally, I have violated four of those, and I'm not proud of it. How about you?

Blessed is the man Who walks not in the counsel of the ungodly, Nor stands in the path of sinners, Nor sits in the seat of the scornful; (Psalm 1:1)

And yet, since I have confessed my sins to God, chosen to follow Jesus and His example, and turned my life around, I have the added blessing of God forgiving me. In fact, He has forgiven me for so much in my life, how can I not be forgiving to every single person I meet? Have you read *The Parable of the Unmerciful Servant* (also known as *The Parable of Ten Thousand Talents*) in Matthew 18:21-35?

For all those professing Christians who engage in protests that misinterpret the Bible (false witnesses who pour out lies) and engage in demonstrations that upset their communities (stir up conflict), or even worse, who physically attack or kill people, doing so in the name of God (hands that shed innocent blood), I have this to say:

Please love your fellow man, regardless of who they are or what you perceive them to be.

This is what God wants from you: *to love your fellow man.*

Discussion Questions

Presented here are some questions for discussion with your Christian study group, women's group, men's group, or perhaps with the family over dinner. As Christians, feel free to explore and question in your discussions, but remember that at the end of the day, it is the word of God in the Holy Bible that is our ultimate authority.

Question #1

Has this book brought you a new understanding of John 3:16 or John 14:6? If so, in what way has your understanding changed? Does this new understanding give you a sense of growing closer to God?

Question #2

When you see Christian groups protesting in public at stores, funerals, schools, etc., how does that make you feel? Has it made you feel like you were missing something important in the Bible?

Has it made you feel like pulling back from your church or faith? After reading the arguments in this book, do you still think there is any biblical scripture that does encourage such public protests?

Question #3

Using the New Testament, what is the instruction given to us when a brother or sister is living a life sinfully? How do you think it is best to approach a close family member about such a matter? How do you think it is best to approach an acquaintance about such a matter?

Question #4

In the discussion of the word "belief", we learned that to believe in Jesus is to follow his example. What example is this? Please don't just quote doctrine, examine this question in the context of your own life. In what specific ways do you *believe*?

Question #5

I have argued that God loves everyone, including sinners - thankfully! But how is it that God can love us if we are sinners? Is not a sinner someone who has offended God? God loves us unconditionally not for who we are, but because of who He is. In Romans 5:8 we read, "But God demonstrates his own love for us in this: While we were still sinners, Christ died for us." In 1 John 4:9-11 we read, *"This is how God showed his love among us: He sent his one and only Son into the world that we might live through him. This is love: not that we loved God, but that he loved us and sent his Son as an atoning sacrifice for our sins. Dear friends, since God so loved us, we also ought to love one another."* Who have you not loved those God *has* loved? If they are good enough for God, why are they not good enough for you? What changes does this understanding compel you to make in your own life?

Question #6

We are offered salvation by grace so that we do not "perish" here and now in the world or in the afterlife. Has there ever been a time in your life when you strayed from your relationship with God and found that you were perishing? Did that turn around when you returned your attention to your relationship with God? Share your stories with each other and see the truly life-altering power of His love.

Question #7

The passage of John 14:6 is a summation by Jesus, whom I have often thought of as The Great Distiller: one who can take the complex and make it simple. What other passages could be called a summation? What is that passage summarizing? What does that mean to you in your everyday life?

Question #8

Has your pride ever made you puff yourself up? Have you ever gotten all tingly and unable to stop smiling when someone complimented your looks or your work? Have you ever stolen something? Have you ever taken credit for something that someone else has done? Have you ever had a naughty thought about someone you found very appealing? Have you ever gotten angry with your parents and said something unkind to them? Have you ever said something that was untrue? Have you ever gossiped about someone or taken delight in another's troubles? Have you ever

78

stuck your finger in someone else's pot and stirred things up? Have you ever thought that you were better than someone else because you are a Christian and they are not?

All of these things are a sin and yet, God has forgiven you for them — for all of your sins. If God has forgiven you for so much, how can you not forgive anyone that has wronged you? Is there someone in your life that you need to forgive? Will you?

Jim Melanson

Poet, programmer, procrastinator, sci-fi geek, coffee snob, actor, and writer.

A devoted Christian, Jim is a quiet and thoughtful man who tends to think deeply and act slowly. Much of this inner reflection and self-assessment shows up in his writing. "Capturing what truly motivates us," is how Jim describes his approach to both fiction and non-fiction. This author has a direct and sometimes *in-your-face* manner of writing. He tries to always use conversational language and make complex ideas understandable.

Jim read his first novel, by Laura Ingalls Wilder, at the age of eight; this began his love affair with the written word. Jim's first foray into personal writing, as a child, was poetry. These and other poetic scribblings provided the content for his first book, *I Apologize for Nothing*, published in April 2014.

Life, a child, a career with the Police Service, and a part-time business authoring software all got in the way of pursuing his desire to write. In 2013, Jim decided to pursue his creative yearnings, and he began writing for pleasure. Drawing on a solid work ethic from his experience authoring technical manuals and writing business proposals, Jim found writing for himself to be liberating and enjoyable. While working on his first fiction novel, he kept getting sidetracked by other ideas. He dusted off an old stage play he had written and published it under the title, *Mama's Slippers*, with the hopes of attracting production interest. In addition to non-fiction works on Christian topics, Jim also works on science fiction projects, including short stories and flash stories.

Originally hailing from the East Coast, Jim now lives just outside Cobourg, ON, with his two cats, Martin and Lewis.

End Notes

[1] Westboro Baptist Church. (2017, February 10). WEEK 1336 OF THE GREAT GAGE PARK DECENCY DRIVE [Press release]. Retrieved from http://www.godhatesfags.com/fliers/20170210_Week-1336-Soldier-List-jacm.pdf

[2] Hudson, D. L., Jr. (2011, April). Funeral Protests. Retrieved from http://www.newseuminstitute.org/first-amendment-center/topics/freedom-of-assembly/funeral-protests/

[3] Deutsch, L. (2014, March 21). Five incendiary Westboro Baptist Church funeral protests. *USA Today Network*. Retrieved from http://www.usatoday.com/story/news/nation-now/2014/03/21/westboro-baptist-church-pickets-funerals/6688951/

[4] Badash, D. (2013). So, Westboro Baptist Church Tried To Protest Funeral Of 9-Year Old Victim Of Oklahoma Tornado. Retrieved from https://storify.com/davidbadash/s0-westboro-baptist-church-tried-to-protest-oklaho

[5] Hudson, D. L., Jr. (2011, April). Funeral protests. Retrieved from http://www.newseuminstitute.org/first-amendment-center/topics/freedom-of-assembly/funeral-protests/

[6] Peacock, T. (2016, May 03). Christian Activists Terrorizing & Harassing Target Customers. [Web Blog Post]. Retrieved from http://www.peacock-panache.com/2016/05/christian-activists-terrorize-target-22860.html

[7] Kingdom Identity Ministries (n.d.). Retrieved from http://www.kingidentity.com/

[8] America's Promise Ministries. (n.d.). Retrieved from http://www.americaspromiseministries.org/

[9] Shea, M. P. (2011, October 20). Did John Write His Gospel? *Catholic Answers Magazine.* Retrieved from https://www.catholic.com/magazine/print-edition/did-john-write-his-gospel

[10] Ehrman, B. D. (2005). *Lost Christianities: The Battles for Scripture and The Faiths We Never Knew*. New York: Oxford University Press. p.235

[11] Ehrman, B. D. (2011). *Forged: Writing in the Name of God*

- *Why the Bible's Authors are Not Who We Think They Are.* New York: HarperOne. p.225

[12] Craig, W. L. (n.d.). Gospel Authorship—Who Cares? *Reasonable Faith with William Lane Craig.* Retrieved from http://www.reasonablefaith.org/gospel-authorship-who-cares

[13] Biblica: The International Bible Society (n.d.) The Synoptic Gospels. Retrieved from http://www.biblica.com/bible/online-bible/scholar-notes/niv-study-bible/the-synoptic-gospels/

[14] Harris, W. H., III. (2004, June 24). Major Differences Between John and the Synoptic Gospels. Retrieved from https://bible.org/seriespage/2-major-differences-between-john-and-synoptic-gospels

[15] The Church of Jesus Christ of Latter-day Saints. (n.d.). Bible Dictionary: Gospels. Retrieved from https://www.lds.org/scriptures/bd/gospels?lang=eng

[16] Thomas, J. (2007, January). Who Are Matthew, Mark, Luke, and John? *New Era Magazine.* Retrieved from https://www.lds.org/new-era/2007/01/who-are-matthew-mark-luke-and-john?lang=eng

[17] Sproul, R.C. Dr. (n.d.). Logos. http://www.ligonier.org/learn/devotionals/logos/

[18] Stanley, C., Dr. (2015, December 25). The Love of God [Video file]. Retrieved from https://www.intouchcanada.org/watch/the-love-of-god

[19] Stanley, C., Dr. (2015, December 25). *Sermon Notes: The Love of God* [PDF]. Atlanta, GA: In Touch Ministries.

[20] GotQuestions.org. (2017, January 04). What does the Bible say about legalism? How can a Christian avoid falling into the trap of legalism? Retrieved from https://www.gotquestions.org/Bible-Christian-legalism.html

[21] Spurgeon, C. H. (1885, June 7). Immeasurable Love. Sermon presented in Metropolitan Tabernacle, Newington. Retrieved from http://www.romans45.org/spurgeon/sermons/1850.htm

[22] Swindoll, C. (n.d.). First Timothy. Retrieved from https://www.insight.org/resources/bible/the-pauline-epistles/first-timothy

[23] Smith, C. (n.d.). C2000 Series on Luke 16-17. Retrieved

from https://www.blueletterbible.org/Comm/smith_chuck/c2000_L uk/Luk_016.cfm?a=990003

[24] Deffinbaugh, B. (2004, June 24). Taking Sin Seriously (Luke 17:1-4*)*. Retrieved from https://bible.org/seriespage/53-taking-sin-seriously-luke-171-4

[25] Wilson, R., Dr. (n.d.). Sin, Forgiveness, and Faith (Luke 17:1-6). Retrieved from http://www.jesuswalk.com/lessons/17_1-6.htm

[26] Guzik, D. (n.d.). Study Guide for Luke 17. Retrieved from https://www.blueletterbible.org/Comm/guzik_david/StudyGui de_Luk/Luk_17.cfm?a=990003

[27] Lim, E. H. (2014, November 23). John 3:16 is the most misunderstood verse in the Bible. Retrieved from https://acts1322issachar.wordpress.com/2014/11/23/john-316-is-the-most-misunderstood-verse-in-the-bible/

[28] Lim, E. H. (2014, November 23). John 3:16 is the most misunderstood verse in the Bible. Retrieved February 09, 2017, from https://acts1322issachar.wordpress.com/2014/11/23/john-316-is-the-most-misunderstood-verse-in-the-bible/

[29] *Do You Pisteuō?* (2010, December 03). *Treasuring Christ.* Retrieved from http://treasuringchrist.blogspot.ca/2010/12/do-you-pisteuo_03.html

[30] Lim, E. H. (2014, November 23). John 3:16 is the most misunderstood verse in the Bible. Retrieved February 10, 2017, from https://acts1322issachar.wordpress.com/2014/11/23/john-316-is-the-most-misunderstood-verse-in-the-bible/

[31] Strong's Concordance: 622. ἀπόλλυμι (apollumi) -- to destroy, destroy utterly. (n.d.). Retrieved from http://biblehub.com/greek/622.htm

[32] Kroll, P. (1998). What Does "Perish" Mean? *Grace Communion International.* Retrieved from https://www.gci.org/prophecy/perish

[33] Randles, B. (2012, March 09). Shall Not Perish? [Web blog post] Retrieved from https://billrandles.wordpress.com/2012/03/09/shall-not-perish-

john-3-pt-14/

[34] Drummonds, A., Dr. (n.d.). The Word Perish. *Interior Coverings Ministry.* Retrieved from http://www.interiorcoveringsministry.org/apps/articles/?article id=22573&view=post&blogid=2796

[35] Strong's Concordance: 166. αἰώνιος (aiónios) -- agelong, eternal. (n.d.). Retrieved from http://biblehub.com/greek/166.htm

[36] IMDB.Com (n.d.). Quotes for Brad 'B-Rad' Gluckman. Retrieved from http://www.imdb.com/character/ch0022123/quotes

[37] G5457 φῶς - Strong's Greek Lexicon Number. (n.d.). Retrieved from http://studybible.info/strongs/G5457

[38] G190 ἀκολουθέω - Strong's Greek Lexicon Number. (n.d.). Retrieved from http://studybible.info/strongs/G190

[39] G4043 περιπατέω - Strong's Greek Lexicon Number. (n.d.). Retrieved from http://studybible.info/strongs/G4043

[40] Pope Francis. (2014, September 22). Pope Francis says religion cannot justify violence. *GMA News Online.* Retrieved http://www.gmanetwork.com/news/story/380251/news/world/pope-francis-says-religion-cannot-justify-violence

[41] Pilkington, E. (2010, January 29). I shot US abortion doctor to protect children, Scott Roeder tells court. *The Guardian.* Retrieved from https://www.theguardian.com/world/2010/jan/28/scott-roeder-abortion-doctor-killer

[42] Southern Poverty Law Center (n.d.). Phineas Priesthood. Retrieved https://www.splcenter.org/fighting-hate/extremist-files/ideology/phineas-priesthood

www.ingramcontent.com/pod-product-compliance
Lightning Source LLC
Chambersburg PA
CBHW070645030426
42337CB00020B/4170